Selena Quintanilla-Pérez

CHERRY LAKE PRESS

Published in the United States of America by Cherry Lake Publishing
Ann Arbor, Michigan
www.cherrylakepublishing.com

Reading Adviser: Marla Conn, MS, Ed., Literacy specialist, Read-Ability, Inc.
Book Designer: Jennifer Wahi
Illustrator: Jeff Bane

Photo Credits: ©sevenMaps7/Shutterstock, 5; ©Lara Gonçalves/flickr, 7; ©hellboy_93/flickr, 9, 11, 13, 17, 21, 22; ©Kathy Hutchins/Shutterstock,15, 23; ©David Pillow/Dreamstime, 19; Jeff Bane, cover, 1, 6, 10, 14

Library of Congress Cataloging-in-Publication Data

Names: Sarantou, Katlin, author. | Bane, Jeff, 1957- illustrator.
Title: Selena Quintanilla-Pérez / Katlin Sarantou ; illustrator, Jeff
    Bane.
Description: Ann Arbor : Cherry Lake Publishing, 2020. | Series: Itty-bitty
    bios | Includes index. | Audience: Grades K-1 | Summary: "The My
    Itty-Bitty Bio series are biographies for the earliest readers. This
    book examines the life of Selena Quintanilla-Pérez in a simple,
    age-appropriate way that will help children develop word recognition and
    reading skills. Includes a table of contents, author biography,
    timeline, glossary, index, and other informative backmatter"-- Provided
    by publisher.
Identifiers: LCCN 2019034662 (print) | LCCN 2019034663 (ebook) | ISBN
    9781534158733 (hardcover) | ISBN 9781534161030 (paperback) | ISBN
    9781534159884 (pdf) | ISBN 9781534162181 (ebook)
Subjects: LCSH: Selena, 1971-1995--Juvenile literature. | Tejano
    musicians--Biography--Juvenile literature.
Classification: LCC ML3930.S43 S27 2020 (print) | LCC ML3930.S43 (ebook)
    | DDC 782.42164092 [B]--dc23
LC record available at https://lccn.loc.gov/2019034662
LC ebook record available at https://lccn.loc.gov/2019034663

Printed in the United States of America
Corporate Graphics

My Story 4

Timeline. .22

Glossary 24

Index 24

About the author: Katlin Sarantou grew up in the cornfields of Ohio. She enjoys reading and dreaming of faraway places.

About the illustrator: Jeff Bane and his two business partners own a studio along the American River in Folsom, California, home of the 1849 Gold Rush. When Jeff's not sketching or illustrating for clients, he's either swimming or kayaking in the river to relax.

I was born in Texas on April 16, 1971.

My family has **Hispanic** roots.

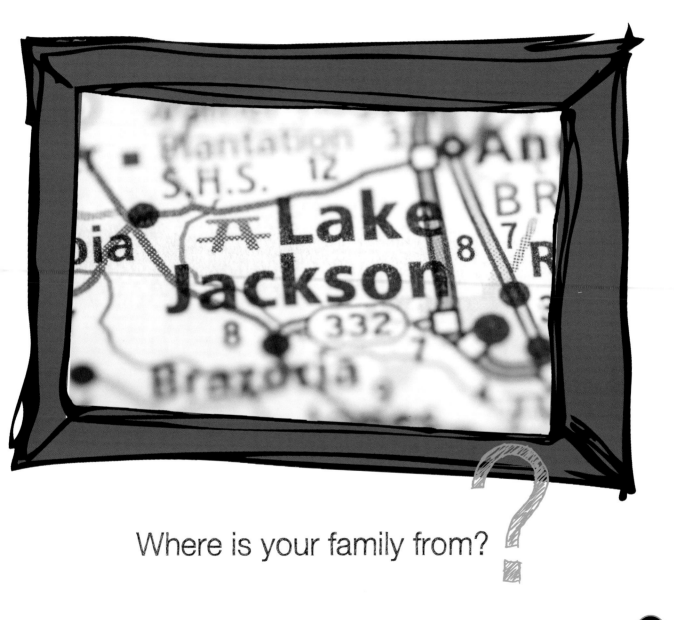

Where is your family from?

My brother, sister, and I started a band. I was only 10 years old.

We were called Selena y Los Dinos. This means "Selena and the Guys" in Spanish.

What would you name your band?

We traveled. We played wherever we could.

Sometimes we didn't have enough money to eat. But that didn't stop us.

I sang **Tejano** music. I made it popular in **mainstream** music.

Some people didn't think I could be successful. I proved them wrong.

I won awards. I was Female **Vocalist** of the Year.

How can you make the world better?

I won a **Grammy** in 1993.

I gave back to my community.

I helped **minorities** chase their dreams.

I died young. But my work lives on.

My album was on the **Billboard charts**.

I was the first Latin artist to do this.

Some call me the queen of Tejano music.

I still **influence** music today.

What would you like to ask me?

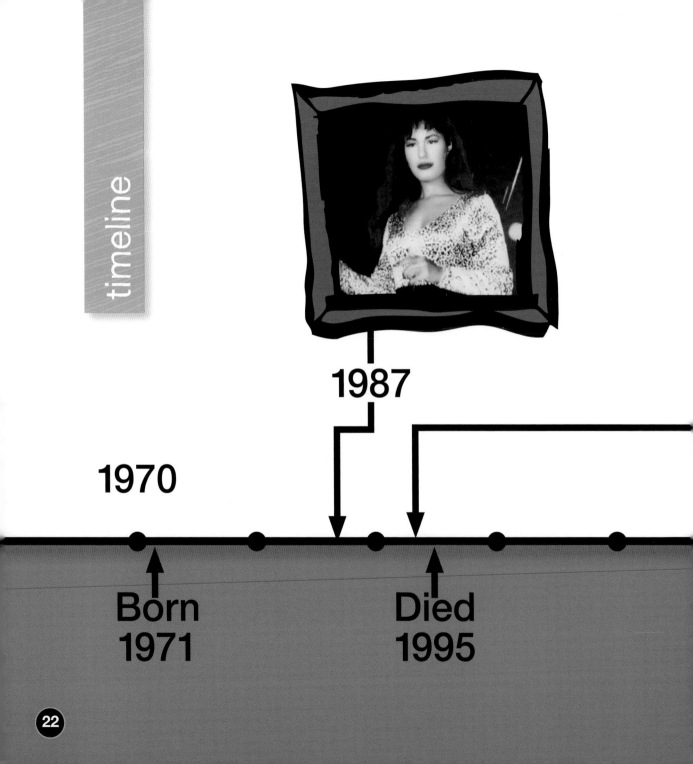

1987

1970

Born
1971

Died
1995

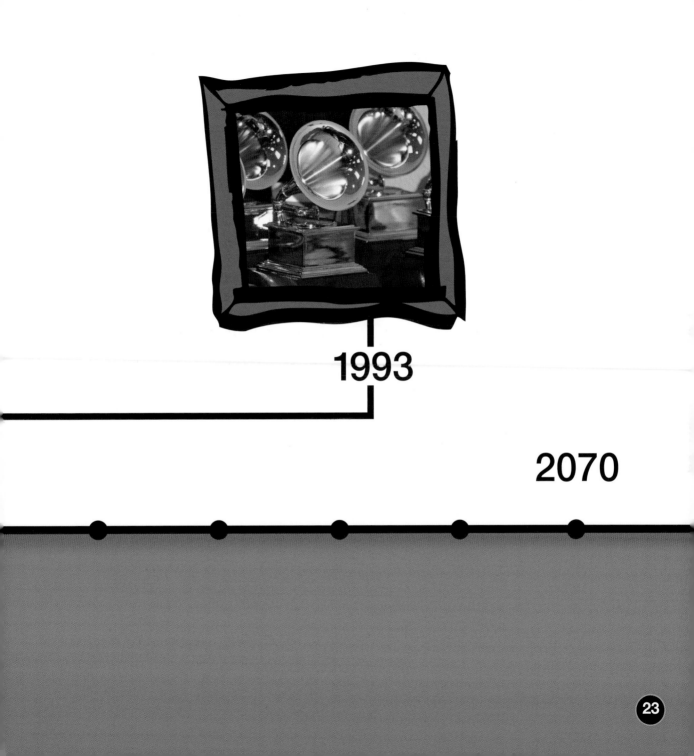

1993

2070

glossary

Billboard charts (BIL-bord CHAHRTS) lists in Billboard magazine that rank the most popular music albums in the United States

Grammy (GRAM-ee) an important award in the music industry

Hispanic (his-PAN-ik) coming from a country where Spanish is spoken

influence (IN-floo-uhns) to have an effect on someone or something

mainstream (MAYN-streem) thought to be normal or typical

minorities (muh-NOR-ih-teez) people of one race who live among a larger group of a different race

Tejano (tay-HAH-noh) music that combines elements from Mexican and American cultures

vocalist (VOH-kuh-list) a singer

index

awards, 14

band, 6-7
Billboard charts, 18

Female Vocalist of
   the Year, 12

Grammy, 14

Hispanic, 4

Latin, 18

minorities, 16
music, 10, 20

Selena y Los Dinos, 6

Tejano, 10, 20
Texas, 4